D0711777

# For the Kingdom of God: A Scriptural Response to a Utopian Vision

Published by Ezra Press, a ministry of the Ezra Institute for
Contemporary Christianity,
PO Box 9, Stn. Main, Grimsby, ON L3M 1M0

By Joseph Boot. Copyright of the author, 2021. All rights reserved.
Portions of this work were previously published in Joseph Boot,
*The Mission of God: A Manifesto of Hope for Society* (Ezra Press, 2016).
Material in this book may not be reproduced, in whole or in part,
without the written permission of the publishers.

Unless otherwise stated, Scripture quotations are from the Holman
Christian Standard Bible (HCSB). Copyright © 1999, 2000, 2002, 2003,
2009 by Holman Bible Publishers, Nashville Tennessee.

For volume pricing please contact the Ezra Institute:
info@ezrainstitute.ca

For the Kingdom of God: A Scriptural Response to a Utopian Social
Vision
ISBN: 978-1-989169-14-8

# For the Kingdom of God: A Scriptural Response to a Utopian Social Vision

**CONTENTS**

# For the Kingdom of God: A Scriptural Response to a Utopian Social Vision

## KINGDOM AND UTOPIA

There are few more odious men that emerge from the pages of European history than the first truly 'modern' intellectual, the professional hypocrite, Jean Jacques Rousseau, famed author of *The Social Contract*. David Hume, who knew him well, by bitter experience called him "a monster who saw himself as the only important being in the universe." Voltaire thought him "a monster of vanity and vileness." Diderot, after knowing him for many years described him as "deceitful, vain as Satan, ungrateful, cruel, hypocritical, and full of malice." He is perhaps most tellingly summed up in the words of the woman who he claimed was his only love, Sophie d' Houdetot. In old age she said "He was ugly enough to frighten me and love did not make him more attractive. But he was a pathetic figure and I treated him with gentleness and kindness. He was an interesting madman."[1] Following Plato, Rousseau was a utopian dreamer, yet without doubt was a debauched narcissist who, whilst presuming to lecture others on education, family and state, abandoned all five of his own children in infancy to a hospice where they almost certainly died. Yet in many ways, despite his infantile and vile character, his masochism and exhibitionism, his thought paved the way for the French Revolution and influenced the Russian Revolution, as well as playing a real role in inspiring both communist and fascist regimes in the twentieth century. He was an intellectual forerunner of Karl Marx and saw in the state the key to Utopia. The historian Paul Johnson has written:

> Rousseau's state is not merely authoritarian: it is also totalitarian, since it orders every aspect of human activity, thought included. Under the social contract, the individual was obliged to "alienate himself, with all his rights, to the whole community" (i.e., the state) … The function of the social contract, and the state it brought into being, was to make man whole again: "Make man one, and you will make him as happy as he can be".… You must, therefore, treat citizens as children and control their upbringing and thoughts, planting, "the social law in the bottom of their hearts." They then become "social men by their natures and citizens by their inclinations; they will be one, they will be good, they will be happy, and their happiness will be that of the republic".… He did not use the word 'brainwash,' but he wrote: "Those who control a people's opinions control its actions."

> Such control is established by treating citizens, from infancy, as children of the state, trained to "consider themselves only in their relationship to the body of the state" …he moved the political process to the very centre of human existence, by making the legislator, who is also a pedagogue, into the new Messiah, capable of solving all human problems by creating New Men.[2]

When considering this, one immediately recognizes how 'modern' Rousseau is and how his utopian thought has so decisively shaped our political and social order. Today's cultural Marxists who are busy with their ideological subversion and demoralization of the West in the name of social justice, have Rousseau to thank for their core ideas. It is therefore of tremendous concern when anti-Christian utopianism is imported into ostensibly Christian cultural theology in the name of the reign or kingdom of God – here a socio-political religion replaces Christianity. When developing a distinctly Christian political vision it is imperative that Christians understand the difference between utopianism and the kingdom of God, lest they be found advancing the cause of other gods and another faith.

## THE UTOPIAN IMPERATIVE

The term *Utopia* originates with Thomas More's ideal society, and it means "no place." More, who was sainted by the Roman Catholic church in 1935, was far from biblical in his thinking. His famous treatise is a plea for the abolition of private property and the establishment of communism. More's work is anti-Christian and subversive to the church positing 'nature' as the measure of reality and virtue, and the state as man's re-creator, provider and preserver. As for all utopians, *unity* was More's supreme virtue. Peace comes through the state – the humanly-wrought oneness into which man is absorbed. More saw himself as an elite ruler in a new order in which men would be manipulated to remove all social divisions. It is not surprising that Lenin found inspiration in More's ideas.[3]

True Christian orthodoxy *cannot* produce such utopian illusions. The creator, redeemer God, in his complete word, has declared the future of his Kingdom and rule, established by his will and power. Since God governs history, the Christian, in faith, obedience and confidence, moves toward God's predestined and ordained future (Eph. 1:3–14; Prov. 16:4). The triune, sovereign Lord, who by his providence and power sustains all things (Heb. 1:1–3), is the one in whom the Christian trusts. Bereft of such security, the non-believer must posit an entirely different worldview. Utopianism, which denies God's sovereign and predestinating purpose, is more than a political idea; it is a philosophy of life, a religious theology. Instead of seeing man's environment as a good (though fallen) creation under the providence of God, utopianism perceives man to be in a chaotic universe that perpetually threatens to crush him. The noted British utopian dreamer, Julian Huxley, encapsulates the modern humanistic temper:

> So far as we can see [the universe] rules itself...even if a god does exist behind or above the universe as we experience it, we can have no knowledge of such a power: the actual gods of historical religions are only the personifications of impersonal facts of nature and of facts of our inner mental life.[4]

In this view, 'nature' is as capricious as the pagan gods

of Greco-Roman mythology or as man's own inner life of evil thoughts. As Thomas Molnar puts it, "our vision of the universe inevitably influences our vision of society and, hence, our organization of society. If the universe is hostile to us, we conceive of society, our little universe, as also hostile."[5] Having jettisoned the God of the Bible, utopians are confronted by a threatening world of flux – perpetual change without a source of constancy. They see no God to give purpose, direction and order to life. This world of chaos in which man's 'freedom' runs wild jeopardizes its own existence by its unpredictability. Man lives in terror, a victim of fate and full of self-pity. In a world without God man experiences an insatiable desire for control, rooted in the hope that man can be liberated from unpredictability into the true freedom of necessity! As J. B. S. Haldane, a Marxist utopian, put it, "There is no supernatural and nothing metaphysical...freedom is the recognition of necessity. This is a paradox, but a truth."[6] But when man theoretically frees himself from the sovereignty of God, he quickly discovers a serious problem: absolute autonomy (self-law) leads logically to total anarchy of thought and to social chaos. Since chaos is not a tolerable basis for a civilization, to avoid this disaster the individual is inevitably plunged into a *collectivity* that will *assume the role* of God in creating, predestinating, saving, guiding and providing for the newly liberated man. The new man-god is the collective agency for organizing man's liberty and salvation. This collective divinity is a Nebuchadnezzar-sized idol that steadily *lays claim to all the attributes of the God it has replaced*. The utopian devotee may not seem religious, since he rarely mentions God, judgement, salvation, heaven or hell. But he constantly formulates new doctrines, ceremonies and sacrifices.

Huxley, the key writer of UNESCO's founding framework document, is explicit:

> If we translate salvation into terms of this world, we find that it means achieving *harmony* between different parts of our nature, including its subconscious depths and its rarely touched heights, and also achieving some satisfactory relation of adjustment between ourselves and the outer world, including not only the world of nature, but the social world of man. I believe it to be possible to "achieve salvation" in this sense, and right to aim at doing so, just as I believe it possible and valuable to achieve a sense of union with something bigger than our ordinary selves, even if that something be not a god but an extension of our narrow core to include in a single grasp ranges of outer experience and inner nature on which we do not ordinarily draw.[7]

Huxley blends secular terminology with the language of pagan spirituality. The union with something bigger than the self is the whole, the one, the ideal of man divinized in and by his unification with himself (nature). Huxley goes on to argue that purpose lies in 'science', namely the endless possibilities of the evolution of man by socialization, organization and technology, through which man gains *power over nature* (himself) to deliver and save himself from suffering and pain, (intolerable to all utopians, including those found in Eastern and pagan spirituality). The possible implications of such a utopian vision were foreseen by George Orwell in his dystopian novel *1984*, where he envisages the problem confronting all Utopian dreams – fallen man's *missdirected* exercise of power is demonic – only power for the sake of power is expressed when man usurps the prerogatives of God. Orwell has O'Brien declare in a noted passage:

> Power is in inflicting pain and humiliation. Power is in tearing human minds to pieces and putting them together again in new shapes of your own choosing. Do you begin to see, then, what Kind of world we are creating? It is the exact opposite of the stupid hedonistic Utopias that the old reformers imagined. A world of fear and treachery and torment, a world of trampling and being trampled upon, a world which will grow not less, but more merciless as it refines itself. Progress in our world will be progress toward more pain...already we are breaking down the habits of thought which have survived from before the revolution. We have cut the links between child and parent, and between man and man, and between man and woman. No one dares trust a wife or a child, or a friend any longer. But in the future there will be no wives and no friends. Children will be taken from their mothers at birth, as one takes eggs from a hen. The sex instinct will be eradicated. Procreation will be an annual formality like the renewal of a ration card...there will be no loyalty except loyalty toward the party. There will be no love except the love of Big Brother...there will be no art, no literature, no science. When we are omnipotent we shall have no more need of science. There will be no distinction between beauty and ugliness. There will be no curiosity, no employment of the process of life. All competing pleasures will be destroyed. But always – do not forget this Winston – always there will be the intoxication of power, constantly increasing and constantly growing subtler. Always at every moment, there will be the thrill of victory, the sensation of trampling on the enemy who is helpless.

> If you want a picture of the future, imagine a boot
> stamping on a human face – forever.[8]

Here we have a powerful image of man's sin coming to self-conscious realization where man, as the new divinity, gains the sensation of pseudo-omnipotence in the collectivist order. Playing at God, total terror and total destruction are the reality as the new man-god brings his perverse wrath to bear on the world. This is his route to godhood – the exercise of naked power. In a twist of morbid irony, Orwell demonstrates that power presupposes, and indeed requires, hierarchy, something that the utopian often overlooks in his pursuit of equality and unity. For power is the capacity to act, to effect a change on something, and the exercise of power necessarily requires an *other* to be acted upon. Whenever man sets out on a utopian project, he always starts with the anarchistic rejection of God and then proceeds to a re-making of man as nature (god) incarnate through the Parliament of man, the federation of the world, as Tennyson referred to it. The solution to man's disunity, his alienation from himself, is therefore seen in a collectivist order, and ultimately a world-state.

This concept reflects more than mere idealism or minor a sub-stratum of Western thought. It appears as a logical necessity born of a lasting, deep religious hunger in those who have rejected the God of Scripture. Man needs order, certainty and salvation, and where Christ's governance is denied, man will attempt to mimic it. Wherever man has denied or rejected the transcendent God and sought instead an immanentized source and root of power, a *theology of state* has developed, and a new doctrine of God has been fleshed out. Although explicitly theological language is often jettisoned, the new doctrine is expressed in the terminology of the social or scientific revolutionary or in that of the new occultist spirituality. All that impedes the utopian revolution is the propaganda of priests, the family and the church. Consequently, orthodox Christianity is seen as the ultimate enemy of utopia. As J. L. Talmon expressed it, "The messianic trends [of the nineteenth century] considered Christianity as arch enemy…their own message of salvation was utterly incompatible with the true Christian doctrine, that of original sin, with its vision of history as the story of the fall, and its denial of man's power to attain salvation by his own exertions."[9] So, man has replaced Christ and his word, and needs a new doctrine of God and a new word. In this re-imagining process, he transfers the key attributes of God to man and his agencies. Because man is a sinner, these utopian schemes must always be dystopian in their outcomes. Let us now examine why.

# A New Doctrine of God:
# The Unity of the Utopian Godhead

## JUSTICE

Utopian literature was one of the key markers of the beginning of the modern age, though Plato's *Republic* is basic to all such modern utopias. From Thomas More to Sir Francis Bacon, Tommaso Campanella and James Harrington, man dreamt of restoring paradise to the earth. The essential ingredient in making this a reality is that the state (personified by elite philosopher-kings) must be allowed to 'organize' society through technology (power) and scientific socialism, in terms of man's new conception of *justice*, which now means liberation from God. Justice is no longer located in God and his law, but in radical egalitarian levelling as the route to reunification. Where differences exist to any degree, this unity cannot be achieved. But why is inequality, moral differentiation, diversity and variety such a horror to man's utopian aspirations?

First, we must notice that the doctrine of God is inescapable. If man pretends God is dead, his need for the doctrine of God does not disappear, it is merely transferred from the transcendent to the immanent (within the world) realm. Now central to the doctrine of God is the *unity* of the godhead, for God cannot be divided against himself! In the Christian faith, as revealed in scripture and summarized in the ecumenical creeds of the church, we believe in one God in three persons in perfect relational unity, fully representative of each other, and equally ultimate. Satanically inspired thought always counterfeits these doctrines because they are inescapable categories to man as God's image-bearer. So interestingly, both the doctrine of God and the kingdom of God are counterfeited in utopianism. Second, the idea of *alienation* is critical to the utopian worldview because it suggests man is alienated from his true being. This idea is not new. It is as old as ancient Greek philosophy. In Plato and Aristotle, we are offered the form/matter scheme. According to Plato Form or Idea produces the copies in the tangible world which are increasingly imperfect in proportion to their distance from the original.

Man is therefore alienated from the *idea* of man and as such cannot find unity with or within himself. Hegel's philosophy is critically important here in understanding the development of this concept in the West: Hegel's system regards man as condemned to externalize himself, to cease being pure consciousness. Every interpersonal relationship, every relationship with the state, every economic relationship and every relationship with God and religion is reification (objectivization) of man's subjective essence.[10] Here, man is steadily alienated from his true godhood simply by consciousness of anything outside himself – the essence of self being pure spirit or pure consciousness. This same idea is central to Buddhism and Hinduism, in which the goal of existence is re-absorption in the *one*, Brahma or Nirvana. The goal of pantheistic meditation (i.e., yoga) is to recognize the ultimate oneness and unity of all things, that distinctions are mere illusions. In Buddhism, the ultimate goal is pure consciousness which is unconsciousness – the annihilation of the idea of self altogether. Thus, in Hegel, West meets East intellectually, although the implications are developed in different ways. Hegel saw the differentiation manifest in history and the created order as scattered bits of 'god' (human consciousness, pure spirit) everywhere. Therefore, man can only realize himself (discover his godhood) by *reunification with the fragmented self.*

The quintessential utopian – and early disciple of Hegel – Karl Marx claimed to have solved this problem of fragmentation within the communist society. Marx held that man was alienated from nature (himself), but could become one with it through work, an action of *nature* manifesting itself through man. Nature is the object and man the subject, so a history created and controlled by industry was thought to reconcile subject and object (oneness). Nature (god) recreates itself by man's work, which expresses his *one essence* with nature. Nature, realized in man, is really god, yet doesn't realize it because it has been alienated from itself by the Christian theistic doctrines of God, man and the world. Man must become self-conscious, aware of being his own creator through work – a consciousness created by the re-making of nature through scientific socialism. When the working classes of the West failed to overthrow the bourgeoisie and establish a communist utopia, Marxism reconstituted itself in less immediate, but no less concrete terms as ecological and spiritualized socialism that seeks an androgynous, classless, discrimination- and distinction-less world of 'social justice' – a world ruled by a scientific, socialist, pagan elite.

## GLOBALIST TECHNOCRACY

In recent years, Marxism has displayed a globalist and distinctly technocratic character, with the pretence of being able to predict the future in a 'scientific' way. The move toward globalism is a natural and logical extension of Marxism, the idea of man's reason as 'law-giver' for all reality and its concomitant totalizing, centralizing ideology. By reason, man takes the world apart by reducing it to its supposed basic material components and reassembles or remakes it in terms of his own idea within the historical process; the whole of reality is to be viewed as the stuff of his creative force. With a global community potentially owning the production forces (i.e., human beings and means of production) societal alienation can be theoretically eliminated by changing production relations. Central to this change is technology. The potential of cybernetics (self-regulating systems/machines) means the possibility of liberating human beings from slavery to nature, in order to live creative lives and be completely themselves. So armed, man can save himself from servitude. Protestant 'capitalist' production relations (i.e., private property, sale and purchase, the biblical family structure and hierarchy, employers and employees, workers and owners etc.,) are a form of slavery and a hindrance to this progress and must be transcended and abolished.

As technology advances, history supposedly progresses in freedom as this 'alienation' is done away with. However, this 'Kingdom of Freedom' is not freedom as Christianity understands it. The progress of history is a constantly expanding range of controlled and regulated acts – society itself being conceived as a self-regulating system. The human being as a societal person (part of a collective) is thought of as the highest product of matter, caught up in a necessary historical process where one surrenders individual being. Only a socialist order (ultimately a global one), can realise this freedom of necessity.

By such a conception of the nature and role of technology, Marxist thought reduces man to *Homo Faber*, man the maker. Which is to say, man is reduced to technology and society to technocracy. Human existence is understood and accounted for entirely in its artificiality – human self-generation as a force for production or procreation. Egbert Schuurman summarises the Marxist view:

> [I]n Marxism, humanity as a species liberates itself, in and through technology, from all oppression and bondage, whether natural or societal. The unadulterated technological-active-historical society thereby becomes the authentic being of mankind. From the preceding it is apparent that for the Marxist, technology becomes a religion. Such a person believes that technological development brings progress that will issue in a kingdom of freedom. The reverse side of this kingdom of freedom is the elimination of the individual. Therefore, the freedom attained can never be anything more than societal freedom.[11]

Working hand in glove with the idea of a global technocracy is the utopian goal of equality, one of those
words which Marxism invests with a radically revised
meaning. If equality is the goal, it stands to reason that
the current state of society is one of inequality – a state
of affairs that must be corrected, and the process involves the development of a panoply of human rights
for groups that demand not only equal opportunity but
equal outcomes for all. This is the ideological root of
all our contemporary 'liberation' movements – animal,
ecological, oceanographic or any other stripe. The *sine
qua non* of all victimhood is the planet or nature itself,
standing proxy for all 'oppressed' groups everywhere.
It is no longer the bourgeois oppressing the proletariat. Nature itself must be liberated in order for man to
re-create himself. This liberation requires radical equal-
ization in order to stop the white, Christian, capitalist
plunderers. This schema alone will bring about social
justice, and all who oppose this program are cast as the
oppressors and the enemies of human liberation.

In all forms of Marxist thought, human consciousness is the supreme divinity. The idea of 'god' is
retained only as the ideal of perfection, even though he
has no concrete existence; god exists only potentially
because it can concretize itself in socialist mankind.
So, "we are confronted with this strange paradox: the
Marxist utopian denies the existence of God, but he
holds that man may become divine or may develop a
combination of purity and power that will transcend any
human form."[12] Essentially, Marxist man does believe in
a kind of super-nature – collective man. This transcending of human form is achieved by scientific and technological work that accomplishes man's essential unity
with nature. "When man conquers nature he acquires

the decisive victory over himself; he possesses himself."[13] This new god, by industry, continues to create. By doing so he believes he defeats what to him is the problem of history: sin, suffering and laborious work.

The dominant utopian worldview then is evolutionary, pantheistic and materialistic. Spirit and matter are one or are in the inexorable process of becoming one. The individual is identified with everybody and everybody is then elevated to divinity. In order for the man-god to be reunited with itself, in order to achieve *the unity of the godhead*, socialization and *humanization* must take place. These *require the co-operation of all men* in all the common tasks laid down by 'science,' as well as the reduction of all things to the secular, to the human, defined by time and by this world alone, not in terms of God, His Word, or eternity. By vague philosophic abstractionism, secular theologies (whether religious liberalism or secular) make the notion of god so incomprehensible as to become meaningless. Human qualities are then blown up to cosmic proportions, ultimately asserting a 'universal mind,' and the results are called divine. For Teilhard de Chardin, for example, this is the *Omega Point*.[14] This is the occultic emergence of a united super mankind.

The confidence of many elites past and present has been in the unity of the new godhead – man. Bertrand Russell, widely regarded as one of the twentieth century's most important British intellectuals, was not only an atheist but an ardent utopian. He writes:

> It is the conquest of nature which has made possible a more friendly and co-operative attitude between human beings, and if rational men co-operated and used their scientific knowledge to the full, then the

world could now secure the economic welfare of all.... International government, business organization, and birth control should make the world comfortable for everybody.... With the problem of poverty and destitution eliminated, men could devote themselves to the constructive arts of civilization – to the progress of science, the diminution of disease, the postponement of death, and the liberation of the impulses that make for joy.... Take first, international government. The necessity for this is patent to every person capable of political thought...when all the armed forces of the world are controlled by one world-wide authority, we shall have reached the stage in the relation of states which was reached centuries ago in the relations of individuals. Nothing less than this will suffice. The road to Utopia is clear; it lies partly through politics and partly through changes in the individual. As for politics, far the most important thing is the establishment of an international government.[15]

Though he formally repudiated communism, Russell believed in a world superstate with total power and a form of collectivism that would involve severe restrictions on human liberty including that cloak for murder and eugenics – 'birth control.' For him it was essential that man, as the new god of nature, must unite 'by love' if the conquest of nature is to be complete and death itself postponed or even defeated.

## LOVE

This points us to the other critical ingredient in realizing the unity of the godhead – love! Man must be made to 'love' all men and for the utopian ideology this love means social justice. This must not be equated with love and justice in the biblical sense which entails the love of God and neighbour as the fulfilment of God's law (Lev. 19:18; Matt. 22:38–39; Rom. 13:10). Rather, since love of the living God is rejected, man must love the new god, collectivist man, with absolute and unswerving devotion. The God of scripture is thus abandoned in favour of 'divine' interpersonal relationships. For there to be unity in the new godhead there must be total equality and equal ultimacy among all people which means loving all things. This means that there can be no *discrimination* in regard to anything. To insist there is a *moral* difference between people and their actions in terms of right and wrong, truth and falsehood or good and evil, as a standard transcending merely human ideas, constitutes *discrimination*. In this worldview to discriminate against anything (except Christianity) is a contradiction of the utopian's most basic premise – oneness or total unity. Anything that cannot be universally embraced by all humanity is thus divisive and to be rejected.

Indeed, how could anything be right or wrong, true or false in terms of truth status in any constant and abiding sense, since such terms indicating differentiation (right/wrong, good/evil, male/female, etc.) are simply labels for different items throughout the advance (process) of psychological, biological and social evolution? All ostensibly absolute distinctions are either illusory, less than fully-real, or mere social conventions hardened into 'truth' in the interest of power for a given class in society. Naturally then, all religions, cultures, sexual practices, gender expressions or lifestyle choices are equally valid. Without this equality, the utopian holds, there can be no unity. Given the idea that all people are 'fragments of god,' no fragment can be more ultimate than another; all things must be levelled, for there must be unity in the godhead. Moreover, since all values are really just social constructs (what Hegel called 'objectivization') in a historical process where all things are becoming one (unity), all basic distinctions in created reality must necessarily be broken down. To draw down this belief from the abstract and land it in the concrete realm of present social engineering and political utopianism in North America, we need only point to the 'queering' of all things as the new social reality. Today, all over the U.S. and Canada (and most of Western Europe) our politicians, having bought into international utopianism, are co-operating for the redefinition of marriage, sexuality, family and even gender. It is not only that the sexual, social, cultural, historical and innate norms of heterosexual masculinity and femininity are being condemned as heterosexism, transphobia and homophobia, it is that the very idea that there are two genders is being denied. The obvious biological and corresponding social realities entailed in the terms 'male' and 'female' are increasingly no longer being viewed as normative in education, law, politics or even medicine.[16]

Politically, this 'unification' in the name of 'love' and care, is extending right into the dressing room and washroom where your children prepare for sports. Increasingly, one can express whatever gender one feels, irrespective of biology, and these distortions are protected by force of law. We are told that there are now many gender identities and sexual orientations. There are the transgendered, the 'two-spirited' (a Native American pagan concept for having both genders inside you), cross-dressers, gender-queers, the gender non-conforming and the androgynous. These people in turn may be Asexual, Bisexual, Lesbian, Gay, Transsexual and queer – it is difficult to keep up with the litany of new gender-identities and sexual practices being promoted by contemporary utopians. To oppose the promulgation of these identities or to offer care and counseling to those who wish to move away from such practices is an increasingly risky thing to do.

In the 2017 revision to the Canadian Criminal Code sections listing identifiable groups (which already included sexual orientation), the highly controversial ideological concepts generated by radical critical theory – *gender identity and expression* – were added to the identifiable groups listed in section 318(4)[17] (this list also applies for section 319 – see 319(7)) and in section 718.2(a) (aggravating factors for sentencing) of the *Criminal Code*. The promoting and inciting of 'hatred' towards these newly created groups now includes making statements in a public place or making statements in any other setting than that of a private conversation. Although religious arguments are ostensibly considered a possible defense if they are made in 'good faith', the subjectivity of both 'hatred' and 'good faith' give courts incredible latitude in finding someone guilty. In the event of a conviction, the offense carries up to two years in prison. Worse, a new Act to amend the Canadian Criminal Code targeting what has been dubbed 'conversion therapy', (Bill C-6) states clearly in its preamble: "conversion therapy…is based on and propagates *myths and stereotypes* about sexual orientation and gender identity, including the myth that a person's sexual orientation and gender identity can and ought to be changed."[18] Clearly here, biblical truth (cf. 1 Cor. 6:9-11) concerning human sexuality are condemned as myth and Christ's call to repentance from sexual sin is overtly rejected. Justice Minister David Lametti explained his rationale for the ban, saying: "Conversion therapy is premised on a lie, that being homosexual, lesbian, bisexual or trans is wrong and in need of fixing. Not only is that false, it sends a demeaning and a degrading message that undermines the dignity of individuals." So, on the authority of Mr. Lametti, God's Word, the authority of Christ, the teaching of the universal church and centuries of normative understandings of the human person are dismissed as lies to be overthrown, with resisters potentially cast into prison. With the seriousness of this threat in mind, it would be important to know how 'conversion therapy' is actually being defined. The Bill's definition is as follows:

> Conversion therapy means a practice, treatment or service designed to change a person's sexual orientation to heterosexual or gender identity to cisgender, or to repress or reduce non-heterosexual attraction or sexual behaviour.[19]

The language of the Bill already presupposes the validity of fictive ideological concepts in queer theory by using terms like 'cisgender' for the biological binary norm of male and female. André Schutten, Director of Law and Policy and General Legal Counsel for ARPA Canada, has recently warned pastors in Canada that:

> This bill, if passed as written, would make it a *criminal offence* to help a person struggling with their sexual orientation (e.g., a same-sex attracted Christian) or sexual thoughts or behaviour (e.g., watching gay porn) or gender identity (e.g., believe they are a man trapped inside a female body) to bring their thoughts, words, and deeds into conformity with the Word of God. But the pastor

or counsellor would be free to encourage a man to explore same-sex desires or experiment with same-sex behaviour. Similarly, encouraging a teen girl to love and appreciate and care for the female body God designed and paired with her soul would be a criminal act. But the opposite (encouraging or experimenting with change from cisgender to genderqueer, nonbinary, transgender, etc.) is permitted.[20]

Aside from the massive philosophical and theological implications of laws which deny the normative concept of a stable, established human nature – a reality that has always informed our civilization and all sane social orders – the immediate practical fall-out means the steady collapse of human society at almost every level, including biological males using girls changing rooms, competing as female athletes and being sent to female prisons. As Michael Brown summarizes it, "say good-bye to male and female, to masculinity and femininity, to 'biological sex' and say hello to genderqueer, gender non-conforming, transgender, and transsexual...if the categories of male and female are up for grabs in kindergarten, can you imagine what's coming next?"[21] To recognize, accept and celebrate these ideas as the highest social values is called 'love.' And to insist that all others recognize and celebrate them, and to require them as a matter of legislation and coercion, is 'justice.'

Therefore, by eliminating distinctions in gender, economic prosperity, ethnicity, knowledge, health, moral values and more, all mankind will be humanized, equalized and socialized, united as one universal entity and the unification of the godhead will be achieved. At this dreamed-of historical moment, socialized humanity will finally be classless, stateless, family-less, gender-less, lawless, religion-less and an essentially structure-less collectivity of beings in harmony with themselves and the other (nature). The imagined equality here is both ontological (in terms of our being) and political. This love and unity, the progressive accomplishment of total social justice, is thus the great imperative of the utopian. We see this particularly in the 'repressive tolerance' agenda of Herbert Marcuse that has become the new orthodoxy throughout much of Western higher education. Those who oppose this woke vision, thereby hindering the realization of 'love' and 'unity,' are to be condemned as phobic, haters, heretics, disturbers of the peace and purveyors of the new atheism – belief in the God of the Bible. Such a view of reality based on a personal, relational God who transcends time and creation, who differentiates, judges, makes covenant, commands, and calls to repentance, cannot be tolerated as he destroys the unity of the new godhead. The heretics must be marginalized, silenced, imprisoned or cast out. This absolute requirement for the unity (oneness) of humanity as the essence of social justice or equity is the fundamental principle of the dystopian nightmare.

## THE OMNIPOTENCE OF THE UTOPIAN GODHEAD

A second necessary aspect to any doctrine of God is *omnipotence*. Clearly, if God is not sovereign and all-powerful, He cannot be God. Consequently, if sinful man's humanistic project is 'to be as God,' then as the new source of power, certainty and meaning, he must be omnipotent. Man as the new god must ape and *acquire* the characteristics of the living God in order to realize divinity. In order to be all-powerful, the new god, of necessity, must eliminate chance, impotence (power-lessness) and uncertainty from human affairs and this requires total control and omni-competence. We have already seen that utopians believe this will ultimately require a form of world-state with universal jurisdiction. It is only in terms of this theology of state that we can understand the aspirations of the United Nations with its ultimate goal of a global order, manifest in the pro-liferation of a litany of international bodies, institutions and treaties, from banks, to courts, to armies, lawmak-ers, agreements and cultural organizations for planning humanity's 'free' future when we will all be one.

The irony of this *coercive* pursuit of freedom through unity should not go unnoticed. Utopian power and control require the political use of coercion with the state functioning as 'man enlarged,' being the ultimate source of law and sovereign authority. It further requires the manipulation of nature in terms of organizational 'science' to eliminate uncertainty and demonstrate this omni-competence. Such a vision is obviously dystopi-an since it requires totalitarianism. This is not simply a technique for domination, it is a religious principle. Molnar observes: "It is a doctrinal necessity inscribed in Marxist theory. Totalitarianism prescribes total domi-nation over man – over all his mental, spiritual, creative and technical endeavors, and its organization of these activities is the *sine qua non* of restoring man to a direct relationship with nature."[22] Total power is then an essen-tial requirement to bring about the new utopia which mankind is said to both need and be destined for. Even if most people don't understand this destiny, the new philosopher kings, the elite social planners believe they understand, and more importantly, know what is best for the rest of us.

To understand the reason for this we must note again an aspect of Marxist theory. In this worldview, the ideal world (from which man is alienated), is the *material* world (nature) reflected in the human mind and translated into thought forms. Human thought is then reduced, by radical reductionism, to rank materialism. As a consequence, true philosophy is not the love of wisdom, man reflecting carefully on human experience, both internal and external, it is rather 'work' or *'practice'* of the human sciences (total praxis). In other words, the concern of utopian thought is not with *describing* or explaining the inner and outer world, but with changing and *controlling* them. Since the human person is a part of the material of nature (all that is) and the progress of cosmic evolution, man is equally the legitimate object of scientific and social experiment. A totalitarian world of total control, of the science of organization and experimentation, thus replaces Christian theology and philosophy.

Whether the utopian delusion is expressed as a form of Marxism, neo-Marxism, National Socialism (fascism), Fabian socialism or some other political permutation, *power* is the central theme. Both Marxism and fascism are totalitarian ideologies; one centred in class warfare where people are divided up into oppressor and oppressed groups, the other in elitism in which the superior must crush the inferior and weak. One calls for the *dictatorship* of the proletariat or the common wage laborer, the other for the *dictatorship* of the supermen. Both are instruments of naked power for the creation of a utopian society where, one way or another, man is becoming a god. In the twentieth century, both resulted in the expression of naked power involving brutal and horrific slaughter on an unprecedented scale. Both engaged in repression, torture, mass murder and 'scientific' experimentation on human individuals, families, communities and whole nations. Whether through the SS and Gestapo, or by officials of The Party, both sought total control of all aspects of the social order to create their brave new worlds. In both contexts, dissent could not be tolerated. Likewise, both regimes claimed to act on behalf of nature (materialistic evolution), advancing mankind toward its destiny in godhood.

The true and living God remains the main obstacle to man's lust for total power and the creation of his dystopian nightmare. Once the idea of the God of the Bible is eliminated the stage of freedom from God or the stage of 'necessity' has been reached. In this stage of necessity, *nature and history dictate all human decisions and actions* with a total authority surpassing that of God himself. These dictates of nature cannot be refused. Molnar explains why: "First, because these dictates are proclaimed in the name of nature; secondly, because man is himself part of nature and of history, nothing remains in reference to which he might say 'no.'"[23] If nature and impersonal processes of history dictate human actions (historicism), then there is no transcendent appeal possible for man, no higher authority to which he may appeal against tyranny and slavery. The new order of unity and salvation is then the scientific, socialist state. The 'One' (nature/god) is totally immanent and so there is no escape from the 'incarnate' truth.

It becomes logical then that to resist this truth is not only backward, but evil. Man is thus absorbed into a *process* that is both necessary and irresistible. Accordingly, total predestinating power is demanded and sought by the state in the name of man's freedom – freedom to be part of nature and its determinative historical progress. In a profound irony, true freedom becomes the renunciation of freedom. The desire for individual freedom is seen as a kind of childhood of mankind, whereas collectivist freedom is to grow up into the maturity of mankind's freedom to fulfil his destiny. In such a view only the immanent divinity concept (nature manifest in statist man), not the transcendent God, can be allowed in human politics, since a God who is different from nature and claims power for himself, would always attract loyalty away from the one immanent god. With man as the only god, complete cohesion and unification is thought to be within reach.

## POSTHUMAN OMNIPOTENCE

So how might this vision of total power be realized in the real world? How might total control, total predestination – the necessary precursor to utopia – be achieved by man? One recent proposal pushes the belief in man's technology, scientific planning and providence to new heights. In the book, *The Last Prophet* by Haldane, communication by telepathy results in the emergence of a super-organism. The social consensus of humanity is conveyed by electronic waves automatically so that all community units (people) act in the common interest at all times. A similar idea is vividly expressed in the science fiction of *Star Trek,* especially in the feature film, *First Contact*, in which the Enterprise's heroic crew engages in a struggle for the survival of humanity against a collective consciousness called the *Borg*. The Borg's goal is perfection, by the assimilation of all peoples and worlds into the Borg collective. The Borg, a race of part-organic, part-cybernetic automatons, are all interconnected by carrier waves so that there are effectively no individuals, or at least no individual wills, although there are millions of humanoid beings (drones). The Borg's claim in confronting races for assimilation is that their power is irresistible. All will be assimilated and 'resistance is futile.'

Granted, this is the realm of science fiction, yet such dreams of a new type of enhanced hybrid human actuate many scientists, technocrats and bureaucrats today – although the dream of man becoming a superman goes all the way back to the ancient pagan world. Surprising as it may sound, increasing numbers of ethicists, futurists and scientists hold that man can become a great deal more than he presently is by the use of emerging technologies that would include cognitive enhancement, behaviour modification, bionic implants and more. It is thought that these things may lead even to the defeat of death and mortality. Julian Huxley (1887-1975) first coined the term transhumanism in 1957. He claimed, "the human species can, if it wishes transcend itself – not just sporadically, an individual here in one way, an individual there in another way, but it its entirety, as humanity."[24] There are many current efforts underway to develop these ideas and move toward the reality of a 'transhuman' or posthuman world. James A. Herrick notes, "hundreds and perhaps thousands of university and corporate research facilities around the world are involved in developing artificial intelligence, regenerative medicine, life-extension strategies, and pharmaceutical enhancements of cognitive performance."[25] The goal is nothing short of self-salvation. As the Humanist Manifesto II makes clear, "no deity will save us; we must save ourselves."[26] Inspired in some measure by Nietzsche's 'Overman' (which glorified self-actualization), transhumanism (influenced by Gnosticism, rationalism, science fiction and developed in the thinking of British philosopher Max More) has become a global intellectual and cultural movement with a considerable following amongst the intelligentsia.

Built on the cultural myths of particles to people evolution, progress, the superman and the power of a collective intellect, the eugenic idea has returned emphatically in transhumanism, but with a difference. The eugenics movement of the twentieth century, exemplified by the Nazi utopians, held that progress in evolution cannot now be achieved accidentally, with natural selection left to take its course, but must be controlled by deliberate selection, since intelligent man has become the custodian of evolution. The posthuman believers agree with this thesis, but realize that the old eugenics breeding program was scientifically flawed; in terms of genetics we are not inevitably 'improving,' since genetic entropy (the progressive accumulation of harmful mutations) is working in the other direction. Accordingly, for the transhumanists, *enhancement evolution* is the clear next step. Evolution, it is held, has produced us, and through us it has produced technology so that we are at the point where we can transform our own species by technological manipulation. The essential hope is that it will soon be possible to so integrate human technology (nanotechnology, biotechnology, information technology, cognitive science) with our natural physical, biological systems, that an effectively new species of man will arise that blends the technological and synthetic with the organic; man and machine merge into the transhuman.

This integration project begins with mechanically augmenting the body, but they believe it will end in an ability to deposit essential human consciousness in mechanical, artificial devices. This gradual transformation would include the extensive use of pharmaceuticals to enhance or alter cognitive functions and would be combined with an emphasis on re-education of the population about human nature. As computer scientist Hugo de Garis has put it, "because of our intelligence that's evolved over billions of years, we are now on the point of making a major transition away from biology to a new step. You could argue that...maybe humanity is just a stepping stone."[27] What was previously considered magic and mysticism in ancient paganism will now be pursued by technological means. Today, genetic manipulation is very much a reality, nanotechnology is advancing and human DNA is being looked at as a possible information storage device whilst many techno-futurists genuinely believe that within a generation human beings may be able to interact directly with cyberspace by immediate access via the cerebral cortex. Furthermore, some computer engineers reckon that our rate of progress will result in an Internet that is a trillion times faster than todays within forty years.[28] Not only is the emergence of the transhuman thought to be in the interests of enhancing human experience in progress toward something other, it is also reckoned to be humanity's only escape from extinction. Herrick writes:

> Professor Julian Savulescu is the head of the Uehiro Centre for Practical Ethics at Oxford University and a leading proponent of human enhancement, the school of thought that promotes the progressive use of biotechnologies to improve human intellect, moral reasoning, and other traits such as physical strength. Savulescu has argued that deep moral flaws and destructive behaviors point indisputably to the need to

employ technology and education to change human nature; either we take this path or we face extinction as a species...according to Savulescu, genetic science, improved pharmaceuticals, and moral education may hasten the emergence of a new and better human race.[29]

Such men genuinely believe that technology will conquer everything from outer space to death itself; human nature will thus be conquered, delivering humanity into the future as evolved demigods. Interestingly, in this process, the Internet is viewed as man's first great step toward a unified consciousness.[30] This vague idea of a unified consciousness is expressed in Teilhard de Chardin's "noosphere," in Ray Kurzweil's "singularity," and in Bertrand Russell's, "world of shining beauty and transcendent glory" that will blanket the earth and pervade the universe.[31] This 'omega point' is a globally integrated, immortal race.

The pagan, religious nature of these ideas, though shrouded in the language of 'science,' is very clear. The ultimate goal is not simply the emergence of a bionic man with an interconnected consciousness through cyberspace. The basic belief is that evolution, or the universe itself (the process of nature) through its human and then posthuman offspring and their technological innovation, is moving toward complete omniscience and *omnipotence*. "Ambitious evolution is merely using us and our descendants as its cat's paw to snatch technological divinity from the cosmos's chaotic flames."[32] Kurzweil has stated clearly, "the universe will wake up; it will become intelligent and that will multiply our intelligence trillions upon trillions...; it is called the Singularity. But regardless of what you call it, it will be the universe waking up. Does God exist? I would say, "'not yet.'"[33] This faith is therefore a religious trust in the posthuman potential, a radical humanism that is fervently committed to the belief that man can transform his humanity to godhood, seizing the attributes of God and achieving immortality, universal knowledge, and unified global consciousness."[34] This faith is also an *organized* religion. As David Herbert has pointed out in his book-length study of Transhumanism, "Singularity University (SU) was the brainchild of Peter Diamandis (b. 1961), physician and noted entrepreneur. The inspiration for this venture came about after reading *The Singularity is Near.* Soon after, Dr Diamandis successfully enlisted Ray Kurzweil, the author of the book, to join in him creating this unique educational institution." Their goal is disruptive thinking and creative solutions that solve the planet's most pressing challenges.[35] Kurzweil was made the university's first chancellor.

Now there is a necessary link between the goal of man transcending his humanity and the need for increased limitations on human freedoms – including freedom of speech and religion, the right of privacy and the erosion of free sovereign nations through the *seizure of power* by a global authority. In essence, to acquire power over nature (that is, himself), man will need total power over people. As Herrick explains, for Savulescu, "more is needed, including worldwide cooperation 'in a way that humans have never so far cooperated.'"[36] Once again global government and control is apparently necessary for man to reach his divine potential. According to some posthuman experts, "the near future will usher in a global culture enabled by a massively more powerful Internet…." Hugo de Garis takes as simple matters of fact that "technical progress will create within forty years…a global media, a global education system, a global language, and a globally homogenized culture," which will constitute the basis of "a global democratic state."[37] This massive centralization of power for the common good will of course require us all to surrender our historic commitment to freedom. Savulescu writes:

> We could reduce our commitment to liberalism. We will, I believe, need to relax our commitment to maximum protection of privacy. We're already seeing an increase in the surveillance of individuals, and that surveillance will be necessary if we're to avert the threats that those with anti-social personality disorders, psychopathic personality disorders, or fanaticism represent through their access to radically enhanced technology.[38]

Total power means total surveillance and the elimination of privacy in order to neutralize the threat from those who have *anti-social personality disorders* or who are *fanatics*. Contemporary utopianism already identifies those who oppose the legalization and promotion of the queering of culture as 'mentally ill' individuals suffering from irrational phobias, and the fanatics are of course the traditional religionists, the Christians: "Traditional religion has been the *bête noir* of enhancement advocates, an anti-technological and anti-futurist force to be actively opposed."[39] Transhumanism is clearly a religious utopianism growing in strength and influence with a real faith in the singularity – the One. Here we meet not only the lust for total power, but once again the pursuit of unity in the godhead which requires the use of power to reach this end. The common creed, motivating a delusional craving for total predestinating power is that "ongoing evolution will 'eventually produce a unified cooperative organization of living processes that spans and manages the universe as a whole."[40] But since the leading transhumanists (aspiring bureaucrats for the universe), like everyone else, are being overtaken by death, what can be done to save them for the singularity? Herbert tells us:

> Kurzweil has set in motion an alternate plan – cryonics. He has already made arrangements with the Alcor Life Extension Foundation to have his body cryopreserved.... Even though we do not presently have the means of reviving bodies cryonically preserved, technology, as always, will be the panacea to gain eternal life – and thus we 'will be like God.'[41]

If ever there were a working manifestation of the demonic urge 'to be as god,' this is certainly it – a cosmos-sized unified bureaucracy of 'living processes' inclusive of the technologically resurrected, managing the entire universe through the emergence of a cosmic mind, a counterfeit god.

It may seem far-fetched that men are seeking the *power* to alter the very essence of human nature into a grotesque hybrid of semi-cybernetic life, followed by assimilation into some form of universal collective, but this is the utopianism of humanism. Decades before today's futurists, H. G. Wells, a utopian *par excellence*, spoke of the 'process of thought' of which all are a part, growing in range and power without limit! Wells believed man as a collective could be immortal.[42] In this quest, man's task is to subordinate himself to the 'immortal being of the race' – all are to give themselves to that which increases knowledge and power.[43] To the ensuring of this end there should be no delay. Wells writes, "My idea of politics is an open conspiracy to hurry these tiresome, wasteful, evil things – nationality and war – out of existence; to end this empire and that empire, and set up the one Empire of Man."[44] This will come about when man gives himself to the collective and to science. 'We can all be citizens of the free state of science.'

The impediment to accomplishing this glorious 'state of science' as Wells saw it was people's feebleminded attachment to God. "[O]ur political, our economic, our social lives which have still to become illuminated and directed by the scientific spirit, are still sick and feeble with congenital traditionalism."[45] What is the solution? "A great release of human energy and a rapid dissolution of social classes, through the ever-increasing efficiency of economic organization and the utilization of mechanical power."[46] In other words, man's transcendental aspiration, to 'grow in range and power without limit,' require coercive political power to dissolve the classes and the use of technology, or scientific control. For the most part, contemporary Western intellectuals (especially the new left) believe power must be used to demolish the traditional family, the orthodox Christian faith and any hint of social classes – only then can the necessary economic transformation take place to advance the collectivist cause.

This Dagon of neo-Marxist technocracy has come into sharp focus in the early 2020s as various globalist and transnational organisations have promoted their vision for the emergence of a technocratic global order and fourth industrial revolution in the wake of Covid-19. Klaus Schwab, the founder of one such globalist organisation – the highly influential World Economic Forum – published a book in 2020 called Covid-19: The Great Reset. Using the novel virus as a pretext for increased global controls on every aspect of life, he bemoans the failure of global governance and leadership in allowing social divides and an absence of cooperation. The time is now, he claims, for a new world order to emerge, the contours of which we can imagine and draw for ourselves. Things will never go back to normal, because the globalists have a new normal in mind for us. "Many of our beliefs and assumptions about what the world could or should look like will be shattered in the process." The unprecedented lockdowns of human society in various nations were embraced with a kind of sumptuous glee by elites sharing Schwab's desire for a technocratic global revolution.

Using familiar euphemisms for global technocracy, Schwab celebrates the massive consolidation of power in 'government' and its intervention in every department of life throughout his book, all in the name of pursuing 'global public goods' such as health and climate change solutions. The 'global contours' that he sees emerging from the crisis are transparently neo-Marxist ambitions that skew reality and mispresent the protestant heritage of the West, in particular the UK and United States:

> [T]he post-pandemic era will usher in a period of massive wealth redistribution, from the rich to the poor and from capital to labour. Second, COVID-19 is likely to sound the death knell of neoliberalism, a corpus of ideas and policies that can loosely be defined as favoring competition over solidarity, creative destruction over government intervention and economic growth over social welfare … these two concomitant forces – massive redistribution on the one hand and abandoning neoliberal policies on the other – will exert a defining impact on society's organization, ranging from how inequalities could spur

social unrest to the increasing role of governments
and the redefinition of social contracts.

The key to the new world is therefore technocracy – not
just the utilization of new technologies, but mankind
embracing the ideas of new elite group of planners. 'Will
we get our global house in order' is the great question
for Schwab – which is the essence of the so-called Great
Reset. The obstacle is nationalism of course, which
Schwab bemoans as a world in which nobody is really
in charge: "global governance and international cooperation are so intertwined that it is nigh on impossible
for global governance to flourish in a divided world."
There is no progress possible for Schwab without 'shared
intentionality' manifest in all peoples striving together
toward a common goal. What is that common goal? It is
to address and ultimately eliminate the perceived exis-
tential threats to Mother Nature, which for Schwab are
fourfold: nuclear threats, climate change, unsustainable
resource use and inequalities between peoples. Planetary salvation thus depends on technocratic globalism.

    The wielding of this total power to bring about a
utopian order, with or without the dream of the posthuman cyborg, requires a vast nanny state bureaucracy
by which the whole of life is managed. The transition
to Utopia may be traumatic, we are told, but it is for the
best. Gradually, various societal instruments of freedom
and power are withdrawn from individuals and families
so that power is concentrated in the source of divinity – the power state. Private property and ownership
is one of the first such freedoms to be targeted. Progressive taxation of income, property, inheritance and
now even carbon leads to open and brazen assaults on
private property, including direct seizure of money from

bank accounts and of land or goods.[47] Money, a form
of private property whereby one form of property is
converted into another, is therefore a means of power or
dominion. Private property must be steadily abolished
because it introduces a rival power or source of resistance to the power-state. Wealth and property must be
equalized and become 'collective property', owned by the
state and a small group of elites. All men then become
children, dependent upon public assistance.[48] The most
powerful social entity then owns and completely controls the source of power. A moment's reflection reveals
that today, the modern utopian is a good way toward
realizing such goals:

> The fact is, that the concept of the state (or the com-
> munity), completely dominating and regulating the
> lives of its citizens, has been, by and large, accepted
> in the second half of the twentieth century…the
> debate of the past several decades has been merely
> whether the state, the race, the ideological empire or
> World Government will stage-manage the last acts of
> the passage to a coalescing mankind.[49]

The utopian evidently sees nature as a source of unlimit-
ed power. If that power can only be properly harnessed,
all the potentiality of man can be focused on the conquest of other planets, solar systems, death and all laws
and norms transcending man himself. The ultimate goal
is therefore the acquisition of complete power over life,
things and people; in essence, it is the will to be God.

The delusions of men in this regard are stag-
gering. The scientific socialist future was the one that
Orwell contemplated with horror. Science in this vision
becomes only what serves man's purpose – which, as
we have seen, is power and control as an end. Society

itself becomes an experiment and an exercise in material manipulation. For any experiment to be valid, the basic requirement is total control of the environment – all the factors must be under controlled conditions. Therefore, in the utopian vision of society as social experiment, a totalitarian vision is a necessary starting point, without which the experiment will be neither valid nor scientific. This is what is said with regard to the failures of Marxism in its political regimes past and present – there was or is a failure to foresee or control certain factors. Having learnt from these mistakes, many in the intelligentsia believe the experiment can now function properly – unforeseen variables can be eliminated. No longer about understanding reality, science has become the task of controlling it.

So rather than the Christian view of reality, which leaves predestination to God – thereby leaving man in a place of liberty by denying the right of total control to any human agency – the scientific society believes its desired social results can be obtained by means of controlled causation. This has led scientists, futurists and political utopians to discuss or pursue everything from cloning to the modification of human organs, the creation of a synthetic human being, control of the weather, elimination of crime by treatment, modification of food, colonization of the universe, development of an artificial sun, elimination of disease, creation of transhumans, forced sterilization, and postponement or deliverance from death.[50] This new tower of Babel seems terrifying and imposing, as intimidating as the great statue of Nebuchadnezzar doubtless appeared to the prophet Daniel and his friends, but the Christian must not, indeed cannot fear, nor can we yield because "The world of the future shall be God's world, and man in that world shall be only what the predestinating power and control of God intend him to be."[51]

## THE WRATH OF MAN

One further logical development of man's dystopian will to *power* is the arrogation to himself of the power to judge and pour out wrath as the new god; in a world rejecting the living God, the need for judgement has not vanished. If God's covenantal judgements in history are denied, man's word of blessing and cursing must replace them. If God's transcendent court and judgement are abolished in man's thinking, then man needs to create for himself a purely world-bound and temporal court for absolute judgement, and consign men to an immanent hell for disobedience. If history is all there is, judgement cannot be delayed. To delay judgement is to hinder progress toward Oneness and unity. As Albert Camus put it, "the judgement pronounced by history must be pronounced immediately, for culpability coincides with the check to progress and with punishment."[52]

The Christian view of reality can give men maximum freedom under the law and need not insist on absolute and immediate judgement in history over all sin, because ultimate judgement and the judgement of men's hearts and motives belongs to God alone. Without the living God, however, the utopian state fills the vacuum in man's craving for judgement. The terror involved in such a view is that this de-facto god, the power state, has no transcendent critique since there is *no God in judgement over it*. The utopian recognizes that not all the population will agree with his vision of a total order that doles out summary judgement against the structural oppressors[53] and resisters, so in political discourse the 'people' or the 'real' population are the abstract group upon which the new unanimity is established. This public is then indoctrinated to internalize the (political-ly) correct way of thinking while the non-conformers are punished with a loss of social credit for their bigotry, intolerance, rejection of the democratic will, sexism, classism, nationalism, heterosexism and a variety of psychological phobias that multiply by the week. To the scientific planners the utopian worldview is allegedly so self-evident that only the perverted would resist it and must be put on trial, by media, politics or tribunal, for their violation of the new positive human rights – this is the presently tame expression of temporal judgement in the West. The brutal interference of the state in the Chi-nese 'commune' system is well-documented (including the regulation of the sex lives of married couples), and yet these horrors give Western intellectuals little pause. Molnar comes to the disturbing crux of the matter:

> All this is done in order to change the nature of man, extirpate his selfishness and instill collective con-science.... The Utopian leadership always claims that its function is merely to facilitate association among equal citizens, including among members of a family – or in the religious utopian language, communi-cation between them and God. Under such a claim the citizen shows his virtuousness to the extent that he abandons the socially divisive attitude of looking out for his own and his family's interests, and with a complete loyal candor, trusts the leadership class to take care of his needs…conversely, doubt in, and resistance to, this ability (and love) show stupidity, obstinacy and viciousness: doubters and resisters must be punished…since they contradict the asso-

ciative principle and break unanimity, doubters and resisters must first be excluded from the membership of utopia's citizenry, hence from membership in the human race. The utopian who has scorned and abolished the coercive power of the state, with its police, laws, courts and executioners, proceeds to restore them in the most matter of fact way...on the extermination of resisters to utopia all utopian writers are in agreement.[54]

## NATIONS UNDER GOD

Earlier in the chapter I argued that a biblical view of mankind and of the state can never produce the utopian idealism that we are witnessing today, and indeed have witnessed in different guises throughout history. The receptivity of many Christians to utopian ideas is in part due to their aping of the Christian message as well as the various ways the core utopian doctrines are disguised in euphemisms. Critically, the phrase *du jour* that is being used to express the contemporary utopian program is globalism. We can recognize its ideological nature by the *-ism* suffix, which is usually an indicator that some *aspect* of life is being abstracted and depicted as its absolute essence. Utopian globalism sees the technological developments and change described above not simply as enhancing international relations but heralding a new era that will certainly lead to the decline of separate states. It puts religious hope in the promise of a democratized, technocratic world beyond war and poverty with universal rights emerging from a pagan/secular worldview. The ultimate goal of globalism is the subsuming of cultures, states and economies within one global international law-order (including supra-national government) with each of us living as world citizens. As such, globalism is the epitome of utopianism, its adherents regarding it as an historical necessity – i.e., globalism is inevitable, and we cannot turn back.

## THE GENETICS OF GLOBALISM

To understand today's globalism – often going under other expressions like transnationalism, new world order, global governance, right side of history etc., – it is important to go back to scripture for an understanding of this vision for human society. In the West, two visions of the worlds political life have battled against each other for centuries. One posits independent sovereign nations/states pursuing political life in terms of their own customs and traditions. The other sees the world united under a single political law-order, maintained by a supranational authority.

The first view, which we will call biblical nationalism, can be traced back to the Older Testament and the establishment of the nation of Israel. When God first calls Abraham and tells him that he is going to make a great nation of him and bless all the families of the earth through this new people, no empire over the earth is offered to Abraham (Gen 12:1-3). Such a thing is never offered to Israel's patriarchs, kings or rulers. We will return later to the reason for that in the universal reign of Jesus Christ – the root of redeemed humanity. But it is immediately noteworthy that Scripture itself offers an alternate picture to the utopian pagan vision that has dominated world history. God's idea was of an independent nation without imperial ambitions. That is, a number of tribes gathered together in a given and limited territory with a common religion, language and unique constitution.

Because of the Christian gospel and the presence of the bible at the heart of Western civilization for centuries, a perpetual struggle has gone on between the pagan globalist dream and the scriptural vision of independent nations which look back to the constitution of Israel. For example, with the Reformation and a return to scripture, nation states like England and the Netherlands broke with the authority of the Holy Roman Empire, leading to four centuries of protestant nation-building in Western Europe and America. In these lands, national sovereignty and self-determination were regarded as foundational principles basic to true social and political freedom.

The second vision is obviously utopian imperialism, which updated to common parlance we can call globalism. This view originates with the Tower of Babel and the numerous pagan imperial powers which followed (Gen. 10:8-12; 11:1-9). There were a succession of imperial powers seeking empire: Egypt, Babylonia, Assyria, Persia, Greece and of course the Roman Empire. Later there was an attempted synthesis of the pagan view with Christianity in the West under the Holy Roman Empire. Other essentially pre-modern attempts at world empire were made by the Mongol Empire founded by Genghis Khan and the Islamic Ottoman Empire (which only ended with World War I). The European colonial powers of the modern era had a religiously distinctive character to the notions of world empire originating in the premodern world, especially the British Commonwealth of independent nations that emerged from the British Empire. However, even the British Empire was infected with some elements of the same virus of utopian imperialism, just as the United States after World War II (particularly with the re-formation of the League of Nations as the United Nations and its growing influence at the end of the Cold War) increasingly pursued a global regime of international law to be imposed on all nations.

As Britain and America began secularising and drifting from scriptural foundations, the faulty presumption was made that inherited ideas such as constitutional democracy, republicanism, the rule of law and individual liberties should be immediately understood and desired by everyone, which failed to take seriously that such ideas and practices are the cultural inheritance of certain tribes and nations emerging from specific religious beliefs over many centuries. Today, Western empire-building has re-emerged with the liberal-imperialist notion of globalism. The proponents of this view share a clearly defined imperialist perspective in which the secular liberal vision of society, enshrined in its radical equalitarian and egalitarian principles for planetary salvation are codified as universal law and imposed upon the nations by transnational institutions, treaties and bodies, if necessary, by force.

The seeds of modern globalism were planted in the Enlightenment era as cultural elites began turning away from Christianity and the vision of the Protestant nation state and started formulating globalist manifestos, emulating the ancient Greeks. For Plato and Aristotle all sociological questions concerned the theory of the *polis* – an all-encompassing religious and political community which envisioned no areas of life outside of the state's total control. In Immanuel Kant's *Perpetual Peace: A Philosophical Sketch* (1795) he attacked the idea of the national state as a form of barbarism and in the

name of reason called for an international state over all
the earth under a universal law. He writes:

> There is only one rational way in which states co-ex-
> isting with other states can emerge from the lawless
> condition of pure warfare … they must renounce
> their savage and lawless freedom, adapt themselves
> to public coercive laws, and thus form an interna-
> tional state which would necessarily grow until it
> embraced all the people of the earth.[55]

This was for Kant the dictate of reason and to oppose it
was to resist the journey of humankind toward a universal reign of reason. Kant's basic premise is that a crook-
ed human nature could be renovated and improved
through governmental institutions and international
law. The ultimate goal is achieving reasonableness in the
individual and finally a world state. Variations on this
basic idea became incredibly popular with the intellectual class in Western culture. A spiritualized form of
it stemming from Hegel's thought sees the movement
toward globalism as the unfolding of Spirit in history.
The "world historical" individual (the leading society)
moves the world toward the nebulous idea of absolute
Spirit. This is accomplished not, as in biblical faith, at
the consummation of Christ's kingdom, but at the point
of human civilization's reunification with 'god' (world
Spirit). On this view, globalism is a dialectical phase of
the embodiment of 'god's' will unfolding on earth.

Again, revealing its utopian character, globalism
requires conformity, through force if necessary. Rational
(i.e., secular liberal) universal principles must be em-
bodied everywhere for the well-being of all the earth;
any principles, practices or institutions that cannot be
embraced universally (i.e., biblical truth and institu-

tions) must be transcended. Traditional religion (i.e., biblical faith) is divisive, not 'rational' and so cannot be universalized and provide a basis for a global society. Jewish philosopher Yoram Hazony has pointed out that:

> Under a universal political order ... tolerance for diverse political and religious standpoints must necessarily decline. Western elites whose views are now being aggressively homogenized in conformity with the new liberal construction, are finding it increasingly difficult to recognize a need for the kind of toleration of divergent standpoints that the principle of national self-determination had once rendered axiomatic. Tolerance, like nationalism, is becoming a relic of a bygone age ... the emerging liberal construction is incapable of respecting, much less celebrating, the deviation of nations seeking to assert a right to their own unique laws, traditions and policies. Any such dissent is held to be vulgar and ignorant, if not evidence of a fascistic mind-set ... campaigns of delegitimization, in both Europe and America, have been directed against the practice of Christianity and Judaism, religions on which the old biblical political order is based ... it requires no special insight to see that this is only the beginning, and that the teaching and practice of traditional forms of Judaism and Christianity will become ever more untenable as the liberal construction advances ... genuine diversity in the constitutional or religious character of the Western nations persists only at mounting cost to those who insist on their freedom.[56]

# The Scriptural Response

The late nineteenth and early twentieth-century philosopher of history, Oswald Spengler, embodies the radical humanistic mentality of the globalist when he claims that technology will place in human hands a world created by itself and obedient to itself – the diabolic seed of his thought is unmistakeable:

> A will to power, which mocks all bounds of time and space and makes the infinite and eternal its goal, subjects whole parts of the world to itself, finally embraces the whole globe with its communication and information technology, and transforms it through the power of its practical energy and the awesomeness of its technological methods.[57]

It is difficult to see how such perverted ambition, embracing not only the globe itself but defying all time and space, could lead to anything but tyranny and dictatorship, abolishing freedom and crushing human flourishing. Such a globalist vision distorts the cultural mandate with human arrogance, hubris and rebellion.

We have seen that from a scriptural standpoint, the root of such ambitions is located in the spirit of Babel, where humanity in pretended autonomy opposes the creator and his law-order for creation. The false religion of Babel – idealizing one unified humanity under a humanistic power-state operating in defiance of God to make all things subject to man's power and glory – is the original utopian delusion. In our time it ends up placing power and control in the hands of elites, banking cartels, multinational corporations and transnational powers and agencies. As such, a biblical resistance to globalism is a matter of preserving actual freedom for real national communities around the world, not simply a theoretical philosophical exercise.

Earlier I also noted that God did not give to the patriarchs, Moses or the kings of Israel a universal political mandate or imperial sanction to build empire. It is certainly true that God's Word is given to all people, the prophets were to speak God's law for the instruction of all the nations (Is. 42:4), and the seed of Abraham would be for the blessing of all peoples (Gen. 22:18). However, the nation of Israel itself was limited to prescribed borders and had no authority to impose by force its way of life on the nations around it. It was to be a model, a light and example, a prophetic voice, but not an imperial power.

Clearly, there was a missiological purpose for Israel as a nation-state (Deut. 4:5-8) as there is in God's providential ordination of the boundaries of the various nations of the world. The apostle Paul made this clear to the pagan utopian thinkers in Athens:

> From one man He has made every nationality to live over the whole earth and has determined their appointed times and the boundaries of where they live. He did this so they might seek God, and perhaps they might reach out and find Him, though He is not far from each one of us (Acts 17:26-27).

This biblical view stands in stark contrast to that of the pagan nations of antiquity and of their modern globalist heirs. Hazony points out:

> This Mosaic view is diametrically opposed to that offered by Kant's supposed enlightened imperialism, which asserts that moral maturity arrives with the renunciation of national independence and the embrace of a single universal empire. But there is no moral maturity in the yearning for a benevolent empire to rule the earth and take care of us, judging for us and enforcing its judgements upon us. It is in fact nothing but a plea to return to the dependency of childhood ... true moral maturity is attained only when we stand on our own feet, learning to govern ourselves and defend ourselves without needlessly harming those around us, and where possible also extending assistance to neighbors and friends. And the same is true for nations, which reach genuine moral maturity when they can live in freedom and determine their own course, benefitting others where this is feasible, yet with no aspiration to impose their rule and their laws on other nations by force ... we should shoulder the burdens of national freedom and independence that we have received as an inheritance from our forefathers.[58]

As such, the genuinely Christian alternative to globalism is a scriptural form of nationhood that recognizes the true basis of unity in the human community in Christ and under His Word, not in man-imposed global political unification. Yet steeped as we have been in secular utopian assumptions for decades, this authentically Christian alternative is distasteful to many modern believers. Nonetheless, the other typical responses offered as alternatives by Christians are simply inadequate to resist the forceful march of liberal imperialism. The neo-Catholic approach – that has been frequently adopted by many evangelicals and two-kingdoms advocates in the Reformed camp – seeks to embrace a natural law theory of 'universal reason' indebted to the Stoics and Enlightenment philosophers rather than scripture, in maintaining some sort of moral minimum for the functioning of the state. This ancient Greek idea of an eternal law of reason in which the mind of both God and man participates – thereby making natural law 'publicly accessible' in a way that biblical revelation supposedly is not – is inevitably susceptible and sympathetic to ideas of universal human rights deduced from human reason along with their enforcement by some form of international regime. Whilst such Christians frequently oppose abortion and usually support traditional ideas of marriage, they lack a clear basis on which to resist the growth of the state in controlling all areas of life and the globalist drive of modern progressivism.

Likewise, the 'contractarians' among Christians who see basic cohesion in society as built around loyalty to the state rather than religious commitment to Christ, tend to view the state as a neutral apparatus charged only with a vague notion of the 'common good' as defined by the social contract. It only seems logical that such a contract could span the nations of Europe (the European Union), and eventually, some sort of global order. Such Christians wish to distance the state from any fundamental obligation to scriptural standards or biblical moral traditions and in so doing offer passive support to both statism and globalism without necessarily championing it.

The truly Christian alternative to globalism, with its scripturally informed idea of nationhood under God, is well summarized by Hazony as a standpoint that seeks to defend an international order of nation-states based on two principles of protestant (Calvinistic) construction: 'national independence and the biblical moral minimum for legitimate government.' This he describes as 'the freest, and in many respects the most successful, international order that has ever existed.' He identifies the biblical heritage of the Anglo-American conservative tradition inherited from people like Edmund Burke as:

> A Nationalist political tradition that embraces the principles of limited executive power, individual liberties, public religion based on the bible, and a historical empiricism that has so often served to moderate political life in Britain and America in comparison with that of other countries.[59]

Since the biblical idea of a nation-state under God with public religion based on scripture is not worked out in detail in the bible into a systematic political philosophy, a protestant (or Calvinist) construction was helpfully fleshed out by the Christian philosopher Herman Dooyeweerd in terms of a worldview applicable to modern human society under four basic beliefs:

> (1) All social institutions, whether past or present, find their ultimate origin in creation. In creation,

all things were separated "after their own kind" and vested with the "right to exist" and develop.

(2) God is the absolute sovereign over all creation, at its inception and in its unfolding ... His sovereignty is absolute and constant: no creature and no activity is ever exempt from His authority.

(3) God's authority is a legal authority. He established creation and governs His creatures by law ... The laws of creation communicate the will of the Creator. They provide order and constancy, not chaos and indeterminacy. Because God's sovereignty is absolute and constant, His law is comprehensive and continually obligates all creatures in all their activities...

(4) Under the laws of creation, each social institution has a "legal right" to exist alongside other individuals and institutions. It also has a legal duty to function in accordance with God's creation ordinances and providential plan, to fulfil its task or calling in history...earthly sovereignty is subservient to the absolute sovereignty of God.[60]

These fundamental commitments imply that just as the family, church and state enjoy a God-given legal right to exist and function in their own sovereign spheres under God, guaranteeing their freedom from interference by other spheres, so also each nation has a right to exist under the sovereignty of God, and be free to serve Him. Since God's creation Word and inscripturated Word do not contradict each other, the purposes of God in establishing the nations and their boundaries as taught in the bible and seen in God's creation norms for human society are all for the advancement of his kingdom.

This also implies that the nations are *ultimately*

*obligated by God to be Christian* (cf. Ps. 2; Ps 110; Is 42:1-6; Phil. 2). No one nation has the authority to impose God's law-word upon another nation, for the king of kings himself, in whom is vested all authority in heaven and on earth, is building his kingdom in all the nations, through the gospel witness of his people in all of life. This principle clearly involves respecting the legitimate authority of other nations to exist, establish their own laws and follow their customs and traditions, without being forcefully coerced by more powerful nations or globalist bodies to bow before a planetary regime of international laws.

The rejection of globalism, however, does not condemn humanity to perpetual conflict, war and disharmony. Globalism as utopian ideology reflects, in part, a deep religious hunger and urge toward the unity and peace of the human race. The problem is that it seeks to accomplish this in an idolatrous way, distorting the cultural mandate. The biblical vision is that all the nations, by the work and witness of the gospel, will find true unity despite their real diversity in and through the Lord Jesus Christ. When humanity acts in terms of its own pretended autonomy and authority to build a global empire it robs human society of the liberating reality of true freedom, harmony and peace that can only be realized in and through the gospel of the kingdom. As Dooyeweerd wrote:

> The Christian religion, linked to the Old Testament revelation, provides a new religious ground-motive for reflection on the foundations of human society. It is the theme of creation, fall into sin, and redemption by Christ Jesus in the communion of the Holy Spirit. It reveals that the religious community of the human race is rooted in creation, in the solidarity of

the Fall into sin, and in the spiritual kingdom of God through Christ Jesus (the Corpus Christi). In this belief Christianity destroys in principle any claim made by a temporal community to encompass all of human life in a totalitarian sense.[61]

The key to a sure future of justice and peace is committing our thought, lives and nations to the kingdom of God in Jesus Christ which has come and will come – for all the world is subject to that future by God's own determination. This is an eschatological future certainty, progressively manifest in history and reaching its consummation at the return of Christ – "for the earth shall be filled with the knowledge of the Lord's glory as the waters cover the sea" (Hab. 2:14). There in the New Jerusalem, the final state affirms a rich cultural diversity of languages, ethnicities and national identities, because the Word of God will have been applied and contextualized amongst every people of the earth:

> And they sang a new song: You are worthy to take the scroll and to open its seals, because You were slaughtered, and You redeemed people for God by Your blood from every tribe and language and people and nation. You made them a kingdom and priests to our God, and they will reign on the earth (Rev. 5:9-10).

Universal empire belongs to our High Priest and King, Jesus Christ alone.

## NOTES

1   Cited in Paul Johnson, *Intellectuals: From Marx and Tolstoy to Sartre and Chomsky* (New York: Harper Perennial edition, 2007), 26–27.

2   Johnson, *Intellectuals*, 25–26.

3   R. J. Rushdoony, *The One and the Many*, 269–71.

4   Julian Huxley, *I Believe: The personal philosophies of twenty-three eminent men and women of our time* (London: George Allen and Unwin, 1944 reprint), 133–134.

5   Thomas Molnar, *Utopia: The perennial heresy* (New York: ISI, University Press of America, 1990), 240. I wish to acknowledge my great intellectual debt to, and extensive dependence upon, the incisive analysis of utopian thinking offered in Molnar's book.

6   Huxley, *I Believe*, 111–112.

7   Huxley, *I Believe*, 134.

8   George Orwell, *1984* (New York: Signet 1950 [1949]), 195.

9   J. L. Talmon, cited in Molnar, *Utopia*, 20.

10  Molnar, *Utopia*, 34–35.

11  Egbert Schuurman, *Technology and the Future: A Philosophical Challenge* (Grand Rapids: Paideia, 2009), 345.

12  Edward J. Murphy, "Conflicting Ultimates: Jurisprudence as Religious Controversy," *Am. J. Juris.* 35 (1990):129.

13  Molnar, *Utopia*, 41–42.

14  Molnar, *Utopia*, 70.

15  Bertrand Russell, *A Fresh Look at Empiricism: 1927–42* (Routledge: London, 1996), 16.

16   For a meticulously researched study of these dramatic changes see, Michael L. Brown, *A Queer Thing Happened to America: And what a Long, Strange Trip it's Been* (Concord, North Carolina: Equal Time Books, 2011).

17   "Hate Propaganda," *Canada's Criminal Code*, accessed July 20, 2021, https://laws-lois.justice.gc.ca/eng/acts/c-46/page-68.html#h-121176.

18   "Bill C-8," *Parliament of Canada*, accessed July 20, 2021, https://www.parl.ca/DocumentViewer/en/43-1/bill/C-8/first-reading.

19   Ibid.

20   Andre Schutten, "Federal Liberals Retable Criminal Ban On "Conversion Therapy" With Major Legal Implications for Pastoral Ministry," *ARPA Canada*, last modified October 1, 2020, https://arpacanada.ca/news/2020/10/01/federal-liberals-retable-criminal-ban-on-conversion-therapy-with-major-legal-implications-for-pastoral-ministry/.

21   Brown, *A Queer Thing*, 95.

22   Molnar, *Utopia*, 99.

23   Molnar, *Utopia*, 113. Note that in both Marxism and Hitler's National Socialism, the doctrine of evolution in nature played a key role. For Marx, Darwinism justified the class struggle and verified his materialism, for Hitler, evolution justified the elimination of the weak in the creation of the man-god.

24   Julian Huxley, *New Bottles for New Wine* (London: Chatto & Windus, 1959, 1957), 17.

25   James A. Herrick, "C. S. Lewis and the Advent of the Posthuman," John G. West ed. *The Magician's Twin: C. S. Lewis on Science, Scientism, and Society* (Seattle: Discovery Institute Press, 2012), 258.

26   Paul Kurtz (ed.), *Humanist Manifestos I and II* (Buffalo: Prometheus, 1973), 16.

27  Cited by Herrick, *C. S. Lewis*, 255.

28  Herrick, *C. S. Lewis*, 253.

29  Herrick, *C. S. Lewis*, 235.

30  Herrick, *C. S. Lewis*, 251.

31  Herrick, *C. S. Lewis*, 251.

32  Herrick, *C. S. Lewis*, 252.

33  *Transcendent Man: The Life and Ideas of Ray Kurzweil*. Directed by Barry Ptolemy, 2009, (Los Angeles, CA: Ptolemaic Productions, 2009), DVD.

34  Herrick, *C. S. Lewis*, 252.

35  David Herbert, *Becoming God: Transhumanism and the Quest for Cybernetic Immortality* (Guelph, ON: Joshua Press, 2014), 93.

36  Herrick, *C. S. Lewis*, 236.

37  Herrick, *C. S. Lewis*, 253.

38  Cited in Herrick, *C. S. Lewis*, 237.

39  Herrick, *C. S. Lewis*, 256.

40  John Stewart, cited in Herrick, *C. S. Lewis*, 251.

41  Herbert, *Becoming God*, 98

42  H. G. Wells, cited in Huxley, *I Believe*, 361.

43  Wells, in *I Believe*, 362.

44  Wells, in *Points of View: A Series of Broadcast Addresses* (London: George Allen and Unwin, 1930), 68. Available online at http://dspace.gipe.ac.in/jspui/bitstream/1/6186/3/GIPE-062996.pdf, accessed June 18, 2013.

45  Wells, in Huxley, *I Believe*, 363.

46  Wells, in Huxley, *I Believe*, 365.

47  This happened in early 2013 in Cyprus, when the state directly seized assets from citizen's and foreigner's bank accounts in order to help meet requirements for a banking bailout and preserve their participation in the European Union. See http://www.humanevents.com/2013/04/01/cyprus-meltdown-asset-seizures-to-hit-50-60-or-maybe-even-100-percent, accessed April 16th, 2012.

48  See recent policy study commissioned by the Canadian government for imagining Canada's future: canadabeyond150.ca/reports/capital-and-debt.html

49  Molnar, *Utopia*, 146.

50  R. J. Rushdoony, *The Mythology of Science* (Vallecito, CA: Ross House, 2001), 25–42.

51  Rushdoony, *Mythology of Science*, 43.

52  Albert Camus, *The Rebel: An Essay on Man in Revolt* (New York: Vintage Books, 1956), 241.

53  For the highly influential Michel Foucault (perhaps the most cited scholar in the humanities today), the Christian past involves the unjust preservation of an arbitrary worldview that pretends to be true or foundational. In fact, Foucault held, truth or reality is merely a social construct, and past constructs should not bind us in the present. Thus, social reality in our time entangles people in a 'web of oppression.' The oppressor class are the white, male, heterosexual, wealthy, English speaking, able bodied, Christians – outside this group all others are victims of structural oppression to varying degrees. On this view, the personal conduct of an individual is irrelevant to their participation in injustice and oppression. If you share wholly or in part, by birth or by hard work, a good number of the characteristics listed above, you are inescapably a structural oppressor to be judged and cast down to bring about social justice.

54   Molnar, *Utopia*, 201-202.

55  Immanuel Kant, "Perpetual Peace," in *Political Writings*, ed.

Hans Reiss, trans. H. B. Nisbet (Cambridge, UK: Cambridge University Press, 1970), 105.

56   Yoram Hazony, *The Virture of Nationalism* (New York: Basic Books, 2018), 48-50.

57   Oswald Spengler, *Der Mensch und die technik,* 45.

58   Hazony, *The Virtue of Nationalism*, 233-234.

59   Hazony, *The Virtue of Nationalism*, 53-54.

60   John Witte, Jr., Introduction, Herman Dooyeweerd, *A Christian Theory of Social Institutions* (La Jolla, CA: The Herman Dooyeweerd Foundation, 1986), 17

61   Herman Dooyeweerd, *A Christian Theory of Social Institutions* (La Jolla, CA: Herman Dooyeweerd Foundation, 1986), 48.